# Windows and Doors

# Windows and Doors

Pictures and Poems of the Forgotten
and Familiar Vistas of our Lives

N. Thomas Johnson-Medland

Photos by Bob and Sarina Cook

RESOURCE *Publications* · Eugene, Oregon

WINDOWS AND DOORS
Pictures and Poems of the Forgotten and Familiar Vistas of our Lives

Wipf & Stock
An Imprint of Wipf and Stock Publishers
199 W. 8th Ave., Suite 3
Eugene, OR 97401
www.wipfandstock.com

ISBN 13: 978-1-62032-116-4
Manufactured in the U.S.A.

# Dedication

BOB AND SARINA'S:

Dedicated to Agnes Lutz, friend and mother.
Thank you for giving me the privilege of walking her to the door
of her new home,and for the gift of blessed assurance".


TOM'S:

To all my people—the ones I stand upon and have in my cells.
You are the doorways and windows that get me PRESENT at the TRANSCENDENT.
Thank you.

"In our religious situation we do not comprehend the transcendent; we are present at it, we witness it. Whatever we know is inadequate; whatever we say is an understatement . . . Concepts, words must not become screens; they must be regarded as windows."

—ABRAHAM JOSHUA HESCHEL

# Acknowledgments

I WANT TO THANK Bob and Sarina Cook for coming along on this project. The work they produce is immense in its depth and tenor. The first showing of their work I went to had a photo in it (from this collection) and it hangs above my desk as a reminder of the views in and out of our lives that move us along into the people we become.

# Preface

## The Combining of Media

THERE IS A SPECIAL place in the heart for images. Some people believe it is in the mind, but I believe the heart holds images as well. The actual outline or physical edges and lines of the image may be something that the mind holds, but the heart holds the deep impressions that we build up over time and the sullen richness of images.

Sure, there may be a snapshot of a thing in the mind, but the heart holds all of the color and definition of the objects. The fleshing out of a thing is held in the heart.

Perhaps it would be better to say that the heart and the mind share the remembrance of images deep within their recesses. That what gets communicated between the heart and the mind concerning a "thing" or an "image" is the fullness of that thing itself. Of course, having leaned out this far on the branch—away from the trunk—I better add that there is a soul in us that somehow also participates in the meaning of a thing and an image.

The thing that is out there in the world has deep connections to many places within us. It is the communication between these centers of understanding and feeling within us that helps to build an aggregate of the composite structures of our belief and feeling.

It is when the heart speaks to the mind and then the mind back to the heart and the soul to both as well that we begin to get a true, deep, and realistic sense of everything that is. Meaning is built on layers of how we deduce, induce, and interpret the stuff all around us.

≋ ≋ ≋

It is no different with the mixing of media. Just as each—the heart, the mind, and the soul—add some sort of depth and holographic meaning to a thing, so too does a thing gain a robustness when you see it across a spectrum of media.

So, you hear about a bird in a poem, you see one in a photo, you hear one in a song being sung across the pond, you smell the roasting of a bird on a fire, you hold a feather in your hand and you have one huge conglomerate of stuff in there called "my experiences of BIRD-ness". It is a jumble in us that produces fullness.

That is what we are trying here. We have jammed poems into the same space as photos hoping to produce a deepening of the ken of associations that you hold inside when you are leaning into understanding the concepts, ideas, and things known as windows and doors. We hope this amalgam produces grace, beauty and wisdom for and in you. We pray that your passages are made more scintillating.

Tom, Bob, and Sarina

# Introduction

THERE ARE THOUSANDS OF places in our lives. Perhaps even millions. Spaces from which we have lived. Places from which we have held ourselves against time. It is not that we are working against this "time"; and yet it truly is.

When we are younger we think we are a lot more solid than we truly are. We believe we are impervious. We know ourselves to be eternal.

We feel there is an "I" that somehow can keep things from passing through us—from affecting the smallest pieces of who we are. We are the islands we believe we are—only in longing.

When we cross the magic line in the sand—somewhere before the middle of our life (before that mid-life quandary)—we are given an inkling that stuff goes through us. We begin to recognize that small spaces in us are affected by all we have passed through. Places in us change because of where we have been. We are not a universal solid mass of anything. The Buddhists leaned into this and called it emptiness and the void.

When we hit the actual mid-life years—the years clustered around our crisis—we have had an inkling for sometime that we are not as solid and or isolate as we had believed we were. We can taste our impermanence in the back of our mouth. A daily notion crosses our mind that we may not exist this time tomorrow.

Somehow, arriving at this realization is at once harrowing and relieving. We take pleasure in the suffering it reveals. We feel secure at the fact we have espoused and gone into the ambiguity we disavowed as youth.

That we can be so traumatized by life would seem horrific and yet we begin to sense the deep reserves of character that waft up and out of a life that has been tried by fire. Some sense of maturity is almost the shadow cast by a life of survived turmoil.

$\approx \approx \approx$

Every doorway we pass through, every window we gaze through has impacted the cells of our presence and our awakening. Who we are is pushed and pulled on by all we have seen and experienced. In the end, the one who wakes up to the realities of their own life—the one who listens for the murmurings "backstage" of their own existence—tends to be a space in this universe that is worn and comfortable. When we bring together all of the indigenous suffering of our own life, we tend to become more whole.

When we come to the place of realizing things come and go through us; that doors and windows are artistic portals of the ineffable, and that transition is really all that life is about; when we come to this place, we will have passed through enough suffering to recognize the futility in fighting every battle. We will be secure in our insecurity and see it - as did Alan Watts - as wisdom.

$$\approx \approx \approx$$

What we learn to look through and walk through in our lives as adults and aging adults is the experience that we would not tolerate in our youth. We can call it the wisdom of aging or we can call it maturation. As a kid, we saw it as the worn down yielding of someone to the enemy—a compromise so elongated in time that it has become calloused soul or empty being. It is not—in truth—it is just how things erode. It is just how objects age.

This is looking through a window.

What we learn is we are an object—not the angel we may have believed. I always loved the image of the terrestrial angel or the celestial man. Saint John the Forerunner is always depicted (in Orthodox iconography) as a wild man in animal skin clothing and wings. Earthly and heavenly come together. The centaur of mythology was striking the same chord of meaning. These balanced images anchor the vigorous unbridled optimism of youth. They secure hope. As a youth I would have hated these very words I now speak. But now, I know I could have spent very little time with the "me" that was then without taking my leave of "myself".

This is stepping through a door.

$$\approx \approx \approx$$

The people that need to fight every battle are the people who close open doors so they can bang and rail against them. People that trustingly glide through open doors and peer through open windows become the laconic guides and lapidary vignettes that call us forward.

≈ ≈ ≈

Dreams and dreaming—these things are portals; they are windows and doors onto other dimensions. In a universe in which scientists are beginning to recognize eleven dimensions; it is our dreams that will carry us on. Old men and young men dreaming dreams and having visions is the luminous synapse of a neural and feeling intelligence that speaks out—even belches out—of the recesses of the insides. God flying out of the human heart is just such a passage, just such a transition.

We find a lot of transition and passage in the wee hours of early morning. Those wispy seconds just shy of minutes in which we almost kind of remember the content and feel of each dream image that journeyed with whispered breath through our lives as we slept. These moments, these dreams, these longing impressions are windows and doors. We set ourselves about desiring them and their fullness all through the day. Sometimes—even all through a lifetime.

The poems and pictures that have been collected here are prompts toward leaning into the places you have been and become. Clearly, every doorway you have crossed over and every window you have gazed yourself through have become woven into the fabric of the "you" that is now holding this place as here and now. The "you" that is here has moved through immense passages. They are all inside of you now.

Reach back and in and set yourself free to bathe in all you have leaned into becoming over time. Journey into the chasm of your life. Stand in awe at the arrangement of the infinitesimal experiences of grandeur and suspense.

You have pushed and pulled—been pushed and pulled - through endless doors and windows of the Spirit. Never deny the way all of that has mingled itself into the one who is viewing the life you believe is yours. It is made up of an endless number yous—that in the end—may not be the one you at all, but a myriad of places to feel from through time. A broad and plasmic you spread out through each and every window and door of space and time.

≈ ≈ ≈

And then there is the "Heschel" (the artistic theolog who most disturbed my sense of being and ontology; my sense of self and the Other)  take on windows and doors. The quote in the beginning of the book is "Heschel" on windows. **"In our religious situation we do not comprehend the transcendent; we are present at it, we witness it. Whatever we know is inadequate; whatever we say is an understatement . . . Concepts, words must not become screens; they must be regarded as windows."** Concepts and words themselves become the windows on our witness of the transcendent.

Words and poems and pictures and all of art are the stuff that get us right up against the TRANSCENDENT.

These miniscule markings on paper and vellum are the thing that we walk through and gaze through in our melding with the ALL. We are developing, building and shaping the very portals and passageways our essence will take when bumping into the ALL of the real. We spin—always—a web that is an entrance into more. Whether it is a thought or a word we are trailing all sorts of beyondnesses all sorts of entry-ways into the experience of the transcendent.

With that sort of glory, who can notice the mud on our shoes or on our hands. Knowing is not enough. Longing is not enough. Being present at it is the whole of it all. We are able to get present at it by making the passages we do through the windows and doors.

**Get present at it.**

# THE POEMS

## The Mist and the Fog

Somewhere in the mist
and in the fog of early morning;

between the place of waking
and the place of
deep,
deep sleep;

there is a dream-full-ness
that lingers
just long enough
to be comforting.

It stays around
just long enough
to plant its joy—

become a friend.

It is the oddness and elation
of a cherry tree
in full bloom out
amid the snowfall of
a December morning.

Something is awkward
but yet, so delightful.

I have seen this place
a thousand times

through these eyes.

I have felt this place
in a hundred lives

through this heart.

I have walked
in and among this place

through this door,
endlessly from before
it all began.
Every life
and door
and heart
beckons me  to lean into the fog
and the mis-remembered feelings
of long ago
days –

of yester-night dreams;

when love and innocence
were the moist-wetness
of the mist and the
very pulp of earth I stood
on to dream.

# TEARS FOR THE DESOLATE PLACES

My tears are attracted
to the desolate places
of the land and heart;

to the barren, dried out
soil of the earth and mind.

My tears run down
the broken glass
hanging lifelessly
from the pane
of the window of
time and remembrance.

Incidents
unattached
to the glazing of
organized thought,
and traditions
not held full-blown
by the memory
have been allowed
to escape
its confined view.

These windows
can no longer
hold back all
they have harbored

deep within.

These eyes
can no longer
keep my tears

from seeking union
with the desolate and
distant places

hungering for their
affection and warmth.

They long for the
one-ing of feeling and being,

of pathos and
the flesh.

## PIERCING THROUGH

Piercing through
the thickening fog and
clouds;

like holding myself
against
the hope of all
my dreams and
the sweet desire
of hungering for the
forgotten content that
wed me to the dream.

That gossamer strand –
too wispy to be a
thread, too slight to
be a string—yet it
is there.  It exists
just long enough
for me to know
the dream is fragile
and ready to fade.
I feel its slow and sure
departure the moment
I see it with my soul.

Whole pieces of my
life are anchored to my
being, to my memory,
to my longing
by a fair and dying
strand that will break –
that is breaking—

just at the moment I pass
through the first doorway
of a new morning;
just as I gaze out
on the vista—through
my window—of a new day.

How to hold myself
in the same center
of myself throughout time
has become a mystery I
am unable to pursuit.

I can no longer
say if there is a place
that holds against all
time, against all shifting
entropy and remains
through all erosions
of our motion in space.

I can say that we will
pass the atoms of ourselves
and everything they entail,
the ALL of who
we have been and
the mitochondria of who
we are yet becoming,
through countless metaphoric
doorframes and endless
imagistic windows—portals
of all we may imagine
or be unable
to yet contrive.
We go through these
places, through these
changes.

I lean
into the GRACE
of the ONE that
writes this life for
my own survival through
the manifold spaces
I have been forced
and I have chosen
to inhabit.

Hold me
up through the windows
and the doors that
pull me from the wispy hopes
of my dreams.  Let
me find some fair
communion in what is
and what could very well
be.  In that place

let me live with
surrender and
diligence.

## If There is a Door

If there is a door
deep inside the inside
of the forest;

deep within the
uncharted
haze and piles of debris
and fallen leaves,

crackling under-foot
- and -
 in the cold night wind;

if there is a door
in there, I have felt
it all along.

I knew it was there
and kythed my way
beyond its frame
and stature -

telling others that, "the
woods make me calm",
or, "I find my-self
in among the trees".

It seems more that
I lose my-self to
my own self and am able
to find peace in
the confusion
of becoming outside
the confines of my
being.

The trees of the
forest strip the
bark of work from my
limbs.  They take the
heavy sleep of
indolence from my
soul and pepper it
around—on the
forest floor for compost
and fill.

It can only be
from the other-side

of the doorway
of "possession by" or
the other-side of
the entrance into
"obsession with"
that we can stand on
our ego and
know its true worth.

Slipping into
the secret portal of
getting lost

we can be our
own true self enough
to see we have
been playing a role -
acting -

all along.

If there is a door
in the woods,

in a nebulae,
in a grain of sand,

it goes beyond
who we have
known ourselves

to be.

## SHARDS OF LIGHT

The light that falls
on the frame of the door frame
is only a sliver of the
ongoing remembrance of God.

How will I hold that memory,
what skilled piece of me
will clutch at that instant
of an instance of the eternal
and call it a "now"—
that has some meaning.

I do not know and yet I spend most of
my days thinking that I do. It is all still
just an awesome mystery at which I
throw my wonder and radical amazement.

I am stilled before His presence.

A sparkle of full brilliance
cracks open the
sliver of darkness
hung in me

against the night.

# CRAWLING OVER THE BOUNDARY

The path to the values
I had held to so doggedly
as a youth—as a young man –
has become almost
invisible to my naked
eye. I cannot see the
map in front of me,
let alone the blazes on
the trees ahead and hidden
like tiny scraps of litter
through the woods.

Focus is imperceptible to
everything in me that reaches out
and listens for a familiar snapping
of a twig or rustling
through the brittle leaves of
my former self.

I cannot find a way
to connect with where I need
myself to go; with that

place I strolled to
over
and over

again throughout
my life—that place of
ease and simple strength.

I am just dragging
myself through life;
trying to get to a border
that has meaning,
to a boundary of
self-fulfillment.

## The Door of Perception

There is a door
in my perception –

shifting and changing
as that so often is;

hidden as that may
sometimes become -

that leads me to
a place of brighter
understanding and warmth.

A place where the
lines in the sand
are understood to be

things to cross over
and not barricades
against change.

It opens onto
a  land from which
we become able
to sit with diverse
things and not be
afraid, but be spellbound.

A land where the
imagination flits from
one way of seeing something
to another—with no
regard for judgement.

This door is so often
nailed shut with controlled
ambiguity that waivers
on the fear of letting go;

the fear that the sound
at the back of the North Wind
is the release of Pandora's
contents and not the sound
of the spheres causing us to
shudder with wonder and awe.

On the one side of this lintel
is an awe that has been mistaken
for countless generations as the
thundering fear of God.

Who is it that sees these things
so differently?  Who is it that
stands on either side of perception,
unable to make the leap
of trusting in the palpable abyss.

Some hear it screaming out
songs of alluring hate and
opaque derision.

Others hear the lullaby
of longing amazement and
crystalline joy.

Who is it that comes
in and changes the meaning
on the other side of that door -
the view from how it is
simply a moment before?

Is it the one who sees that
stands on either side of perception
and changes;

is it the view that is given
to be seen that shifts
and changes its intricacies of
meaning and import.

One of these worlds
is a safer place to
live, the other is simply
populated with more
people sharing the view.


There is a door
in my perception –

shifting and changing
as that so often is;

hidden as that may
sometimes become –

that leads me to
a place of brighter
understanding and warmth.

I will choose to see from
this door frame—into this
perception as though through
the gate with flaming swords and
Seraphim.  I will choose to see
things in the light of beauty
and freedom.  Others, others
will do as they are able.

This is how
we tread ourselves
into and out of
paradise...all the day long.

# THE ONE

In the waiting
that comes between
each breath
and each drop of rain

falling upon my face
comes the hope that
this will be the
moment in time
that I have been
born for—that
we have been
born for;

this will be the
I AM moment when
we can recognize our
place in things
simply in hearing
our heartbeat
or the cricket's
chirp.
Everyone of us
believes that we
are "the one";

that our lives are the
most auspicious ones
that there are; that
we are the one
that everyone has
bent their
hope around and
leaned into for meaning.

In fact, we only
need to recognize
this for ourselves.

The bark on that tree
is the right bark for it.

The moss on that
stone is that stone's
ideal moss.

The self that has
wrapped itself all
around my own ego
and perception of
all that is is "the
one" just for me.

In that settling
thought everything
is nothing more than the
falling apart of leaves into
all things dirt and
the decay that makes
all life new.

In the hidden connection
we all share along the axis
of meaning in the hologram of
God and Life; we are all
"the one". Waking
up to this subtle
confusion of union
takes nothing less than
complete surrender.

Fana is not
a way you can simply

choose to go . . . it encroaches
upon you from
all directions.

This leaf, -
this is the ONE.

## Before the Divisions

Go back to the place
you were before you
gathered images and inklings.

Return to the you
that was before
the divisions
of learning took place.

Enter the underground stream
from which everything
flows into separateness

but do not
come back.

Once you stop swimming
between the two worlds
and just let go,
you will have brought the two
together as one.

Once you allow
that which is within you
to come out and save you,

quick, jump in
and drown in the oneness.

That will be your
awakening. On that day
you will have been
born again.

# THE RAVEN

A raven cries in the morning still;
my heart longs to know what she sees.

Is it a thank you for the food I left her
only a day ago

that is now gone.

Or,
in the oppressive heat
that is hanging all around the
bottom of the trees

and just above the crisp and
broken leaves of last autumn

has she discovered a hidden
ken of mirth and utter delight
at the simple spectacle
of finding a shiny pebble or
some hidden bauble that

secretly makes her chuckle
and feel wonderfully alive.

I am happy to simply
believe that either of these may be true;
and that perhaps neither of them are true
as well.

Her presence,
her caw
just makes me glad.

## There is an Opulence

There is an opulence
in the heart of we
who have an ocean at our backdoor.
There is a fullness we exude
when we live close to any
body of water.

We are transformed by the
magnet-pulling charge of water;

abrading itself over
earth and stone—again and again.

We can feel—from the center
of our chest—the imagined lure
of our mistress the sea;

the beckoning fingers of our river-lover;

the long awaited embrace
with our impassioned lake.
This primordial rendezvous
with our ancient ancestral
waters

is in our blood from
having grown so close
to their dappled shores in our lives;

stirring the amniotic mother-hold of saline shore

and deep cataracts
and rivulets sing to us
from within our veins.

The call so strong from
these dampening spaces;
I cannot know how a man can grow
rich
without the rhythmed presence
of water.

I am lured in by waters.
There is an opulence
in the heart of we
who have an ocean at our backdoor.
There is a fullness we exude
when we live close to any
body of water.

# The Certain Uncertainty

When I woke up
and was able to smile

at the beautiful mess
that is the world;

I knew that chaos
would settle itself

into an elegant symphony
of rhythm and grace.

A song sung out
in silent reverberation;

a tune made whole
on melodious emptiness.

There is a something
in the nothingness of
space and time.

There is a something
that lures you out;

calling you just over
a barely visible line

in the sands of time

that somehow are your
life; and the
cumbersome pieces of what
used to be your past.

Old worn out hiking boots
are seen in the shadow—

mingled hideously
and unpretentiously with
dried rose petals
from Eliot's  bowl and
dust and the passage of
time.

Warp and weft tell
it all.

# THE REPULSION OF FIELDS

The repulsion of fields
grows in the same rythmed
fashion

as the steady collapsing
of my ego; falling
in upon itself—

in

always in—
drawing all matter in
upon the wake of its
own collapsing.

A similar opposition
of the repulsion of

all fields.

Behind the apparent solidity,
of all we hold so dear,

is the thundering emptiness
of nothingness.

No government,
no stock exchange,
no religion,
no science.

Only a mass of
infinitely invisible
vibrating strings

that sing softly—
just enough to entice
each other into
illusory resonance.

We know it to be so;
because it seems so.
And, thus we build
a world; look through
the imagined window of the mind
and find what we have slowly
woven into truth.

A nautilus knows something
of its wholeness throughout;

even from its innermost chamber.

The ripples
on the pond
somehow share the
tale of their beginning

with the first-fall of
the pebble on the stillness.

## ACHE OF THE FAMILIAR

Rarely does a person
escape childhood
without learning something
so well
as to cause a pain
in adulthood.

Aching
for the familial impression
of the familiar
that once was strong
but is now so faint
as to be only
the remembrance of
the smell of roasting
garlic and tomatoes.

Tangled together
in the windows of
our longing remembrance
are the ample but not
quite complete thoughts
that whisper a simple
hungering drool
in the doors of the heart
of our long journeyed
aching but steady feet.

We have carried our beginning
all the way into the middle of
our memory and forgetting.

Everything I do
is a simple attempt
at making my sauce

to taste
if not the same
better
than hers.

I long for
the familiar.

It is the way I turn
my head just a bit
to the left and looking
up and off to the
right

that crept into the cells
of my aging—somehow
triggered to go off
just at 35—like it did
in him.

It is the shadow of a
thought process that was his—all
through my childhood—that
leapt out from me when I turned
20, and was in the thick of
my intellectual days.

It is the caustic wit that was
hers that I wove into my life from
my childhood right in and up
to this very day of my life.

It is all in there.

Each and every
one of them

is a clean threshold
and an open frame

in on the me that has become
a part of this
spacious cosmos I now

inhabit.

Then is now.

I am them.

# IF A STONE

If a stone should
fall out from the bottom;

fall out from the middle
of the bottom
of a wall
along the
boundary of a field;

would that change things?

Would time
fall through the stones
into the dirt
and somehow
wash away important things
that we had only just
remembered from our past –

things we swore
as children

we would never regress upon -
never undo our
severity of emotion
and belief.

Or, would it just be
a break in the bottom
of a stone wall
that runs along a field

at the base
of a red shale mountain

just outside Uhlerstown,
Pennsylvania.

At the end of spring,
I believe.

# The Threshold of Compassion

There is always a small
opening

through which compassion can
seep in to a conversation,
an act, a
grudge.

It is a pause
in the chatter,

stillness of motion,
or an easing of the tension.

It does not appear for
long,

but when it does, if you
are not well versed

in tossing caution to the wind;

or in leaning heavily into impulse,

you will walk right over
it with no remorse.

You will feel that
your selection of
the path of stern
position is not

only deserved and
warranted,

but the only way a man can go.
Each time
that you pass over this line,
you will be hardening
your ability to casually
enter the fray of compassion.

## Doorways and Grace

The entrance
to a thousand,
thousand places
in the warp
and weft of
space and time
is crossed in one
instant.
An instant
that is built
on countless layers of
places and days piled
and piled and piled
from the beginning
of forever and beyond
the inception of
eternity.
And we,
we who think that
all that
has only just
happened –
and call that instant
of alleged happening
GRACE
have missed the
foreplay of time.
The true grace
is that we made it
to this time
and to this place
against all odds.
And then
walked through
the entrance of this moment.

Against all odds.
But it is not
simply this moment
that we enter at any point
along the line;
for this moment we cross into
bears out all that has been
and all that is yet to be
in a kaleidoscope
of stretched out existence.
For every instance and
every instant exists
throughout the whole
of all that has been.
Holograms are not new,
they are all that has
ever been.  Holograms
are doorways and grace.

## Confluence

Profound joy comes
from a place where
the confluence
of the rivers of love,
stillness, vast-openness,
and supple lush-growth
is able to weather and
erode the sharp-harshness
of the bedrock of our days –

the buried and upheaved
igneous, sedimentary,
and metamorphic layers,
and pockets of our lives.

When these things
wear us down over time,
we are a people
of sound-depth
and an inner-awe-wonder.


We marvel at the simple
preposterousness of life.


We gaze
rapt in amazement
that the world has
doorways into vistas
of ease and contentment;


places of rest where wisdom
settles in and comforts us.

The suffering that comes
from erosion produces
intense-landscapes of beauty
when we gaze out –

beyond the immediate


pain
and abrasive removal of form.


Our broken-offness
is a testimony to
the uncontrollable
ability of life to
have its way

over and above the boundary
of what we find to be reasonable.

# An Entrance into Consumption

Our venture

years ago
into the world of the
earth;

into the world
of the dirt and the growing

led us to feel with every
cell and with every corpuscle

that we call us

that there was something
wrong; there was something
amiss;

that there was something more
than the average folk
let on to.

My wife and I would
tend the soil.

It was the small innuendos
at the party that would
reveal
the true heart of people -

the heart of stone cold greed
and inability to see their own
avarice and contempt for

all creation.

A word about how we each
thought our lives the most
important,

our ability to shop
far more important than
the issue of
molded plastic mounting up
higher and more immense
than Kilimanjaro.

A backward glance
that was a sneer—more than
a glance. A sending
out of pointed shards,
not a soft receiving.

Each mingling with the masses
that we would enter into would
cause us to return home

elaborating on our silent venture
and subtle conspiracy with the
earth to overtake the planet
with herbs, and trees, and perennial-life
laced with horrid compost.

Our encounters with a generation
gone mad—with its own need for
everything it could imagine
and no shape inside
for trying to resolve the hollows
in the planet as it
pulls out all it has to give –

dropped us to our knees to
plant oceans of daffodils
and tulips;

to rage against
the existential dread of a people

that could not see the nations of
plastic and waste growing
just beyond the perception
of their small and flailing egos;

beyond the invisible boundaries
of what used to be community.

We tried to fill
the hollows with green.

Beyond our
skin we felt the dragging pull
of interior opulence
almost choking us.

Each one a car—
and then 3 –
each one a hose,
each one a mower, a blower, and
whacker.

Each one 4 toilets, 3 showers,
3 televisions, 5 computers.

Each one having more and more
until it become
just beyond vogue,

to build spaces called units,
to pile higher and deeper with the

debris of our own eager
spoilage and despotism of
stuff.

Temperatures are rising.
Colonies of bees are dying.
Limping and bedraggled
mankind is now speaking of the

global crisis.

At their parties.

In their homes.

But no one will
ride a horse.  Not one will
refuse electric.  Few will
till the soil and plant
a seed.  Hope for
the primordial link
is gone –
the proto-seminal bond
with fingers and dirt
is no longer on the horizon
of our capitulation.

The we that had worked so
hard to find a place in
correcting the ills of the
generations is now lost
in the we of us all
that stands staring, almost hopelessly
at the ravishes that have been
dumped on our good earth.

the changes move so quickly
now that they are we and we

are them.  All of us now
stand clad in the same
prison suits of collective
squalor and despair.

Too long the rampancy
has gone unchecked.

What we now know and hold as
self-evident truths

we have allowed to grow beyond
our control

and that will change us vastly.

We run against the tide
and the wind to find
a lackey we can point to

to hang from a willow -
in shame -

for all the destruction he has
heaped upon this earth.

We walked through
this door years ago

we are only just now
recognizing

that the map we used to get
to where we are

had only one destination.

Consumption.

We can still put
things back in the earth
that matter.

We can plant hope
with our trowel,
just next to the rudbeckia.

We can turn under joy
when we compost our
dirt with the remnants
of our harvests.

There is a circle
we are a part of,

but, we must leave
this place of tangled
usurping digestion.

How will we get
back through the door
of an awkward capitalistic
industrialism
we have clumsily

entered?

A door we were
told would
be the entrance into
the achievement of all our dreams.

I never dreamed this
damage.

## Family View

On the edge of Ralston
was an implacable
need to rule and survey
the island of his familiar.

Ellen held fast to her
belief that Robert was a bastard.

Lined along the pictures
my soul holds tightly to
for these and the others
I have both known and not,
is the occasional rearing of
some ancestral lure,
a passioned curse rears its
head and I am want and
disposed to things
I have no inkling why
I am leaning into.

I loved that I loved
Talmud and was not a Jew.
Yet, I find now
back
only a few generations
back through a door in my genes
there is a Yetta, a
Gottlieb, an Isaac and Morton.

I am a Jew and now
the longing was in my cells
not just my heart.

Joseph held his papa's
hand on the boat leaving Bremen

and the sickness I feel
with each crashing of the
deep and rugged waves

is their sickness at fleeing
their own soil and hearth.

The way in to who we
are
this moment
is clearly through
the apex of our ancestral
past.

The window of our
personal us—the we of
who we hold ourselves to be –

looks out on the celestial
map of our being
and sees mitochondria.

The glorious us—the body
electric—is woven not only
with stardust and carbon.

In there,

through the looking
glass, is Alex, Norman, and
Margaret.

Each a world
spun
in flesh and desire;

implanted
in the me that sits

here singing songs of longing
and eternity.

The door in
goes through all time.

It knows the space of
all beings that
brought me into BE.

My love of apple
pie is hers. My obsession with
pencils is his. My chin and
hair, and waist is theirs.

I am built on
Buddhist void of
no one thing. The I that I
thought was home
is legion. The me I wanted
to make myself into
is only them in multiplicity.

Where is the door,
but everywhere.
Where is the window
but right here.

From
the smallest days
of
long-ago
a door I happened on
has become
a lifetime of art –
of images and words.

Tripping
over the blue
and azure words that
would become a
path of tender-hearted
amblings on the underside
of the way –
the way of longing
and desire,

I have righted
myself in the color
and feel of what they
have had to say for
the me that I thought
I was—all along.

A word
is nothing more
than the underside of
longing
and
desire.  It swims
and tangles itself
among the strands
and fibers of

life and jumbles
all its receptors
and contectors into the
main of a thing
of a feeling
until the mention of its own
syllables call forth
such a vivid and pungent
hunger for the thing it names
that the mind shuts down and
man,
woman,
child lives in the
murkiest of muds until
hunger is sated,
longing is  quelled and
desire is soothed –
for a moment.

And then,
a new word sounds
in our life and calls us beyond
the measured borders of
our days into the lands
beyond the frame.

In youth the words are
fields, and skies, and
animals and bees
of mirth—feeding
on clover and
pollens from the
oceans of new spring
growth.

Our youth calls
forth words that

arouse our need
to spawn:
sweat and breasts
and sperm and heaving
motions of the soul toward
epic greatness and
longevity of ideals
and social movements.
Truth, and peace ooze from
our pores like pheromones
of arousal. Our youth is
nothing but
procreation of the species and
ideals.  There would be no
revolutions with out
the pathways of
our youthful lusts
and ambitions.

The days we find
our falling apart
are planted and peppered
with a need to succeed
and go beyond what
we know is coming
next.
The first tug in our
life –
toward the grave –
appears and scares
us beyond the reason
of our days.

We see the drooping
of a lid or the early
morning limp.

It rears its head

for a season, but leaves its
mark of questioning return
on the underside of
the soul—causing an
urgency within that
will not leave until
it has drained each
and every ounce of
potent and driving energy
from the cells of
your wholeness and being.
Onto the life
around you;
striking an air of permanence
into the ken
of our very  human existence
and presence in this world
of matter, and flesh, and
value long lasting.

Passing next
into the field of our
decrepitude and waste

is the failing of the flesh
we call old age; and
trading it relentlessly in the
wind for what we think
we can hold for a moment

is the lasting illusion
that there is one more
drink from the crystal
fountain

that will restore to us the
pathway of our days gone by.

Each step along
the way we cry to the heavens
"CARPE DIEM" and think
we are screaming
"CARPE DEUM". We

can no more seize the day
than we can seize the god.

Our days pass slowly
over the face of the
divide
like a silk scarf across the naked
breast, calling us
further in to the
moment of captured
want and hope.

At some point,
if we find grace
within the haunted mind
of our mis-understanding

we will hear the accent
echo of the uttered phrase

"all emptiness is form
and form emptiness"

and come to know it as
the truth of every doorway
we have darkened and window
frame we have peered ourselves
through,

the underside of what we have here,
just in our grasps,

is empty of all
intrinsic meaning.

Emptiness is form;
form is emptiness.

# THE BEAUTY OF THE WORN

There is a beauty
in the wind, sun, and water-worn
wood that makes a door.  Standing
against the wear of time and space
beating down on it—endlessly from
its incept into this place—worn;
always wearing in the weather
of life.

There is a story that seeps and creeps
out of each crack and crenulation;
a mentioning of weakness and
strength turned in an against
the beating of force against
stillness;
stillness against force.

The face wears, too,
sloughing layer after layer to
give up new flesh;
new flesh a door or
window pane cannot
express.

It seems character is exposed
in the wear. Each clever mark upon
the surface tells a position once
held and leaned into with a lever against
all odds and a firm and solid
place to stand.

There is a beauty in the wearing;
there is a beauty in the

wind, sun, and water-worn
wood that makes a door.  Standing
against the wear of time and space
beating down on it—endlessly from
its incept into this place—worn;
always wearing in the weather
of life. There is a beauty in the
corner where the lines
of the eye reveal an aged
turning toward the weather
of life's woes, and a dried,
tanned crinkle revealing the
heart's steady calm and force
of resignation in a smile and
a nod.

## Something to Hold Onto

A knob finds itself in just
the right place if it is easy to
grasp and provides a stable
point in space for the hand that
reaches out for it.

Many a door has worn itself
so frail and weak that a knob
although most want as a place
of holding can be given
to a corner, and edge,
or a rope. The vantage of the hand
and grip is flexible
for sure as long as opening
and closing can be had by its
regular and routine use.

Every once and a while a foot
is fine for the flinging open of
door;

be it shed or house or barn.

All in all, though, a door looks
more itself when a knob
is finely stationed there for
grabbing, pushing and pulling.

It is an axiom of choice for most
who share the view of doors as bold
and strong reminders that what
is on this side and what is on that side
are two different things, two
different lands to enter into
and depart out of.

It is the fulcrum of the change
and transformation—the knob is.
Perhaps a place of gaining and
gathering strength for the journey
into or out from.

For most, it just completes
the door in a way so as not
to let it look worn or beaten down.

The arms of change are few that
inspire the heart with the artistry of
delight. But on the countenance of
the knob, the handle, the latch there
is a feel of finery and lace, of utility
and frill that let's us know just a bit
about the owner of this door –
the keeper of this way.

Hold it fast,
grab it firm and
feel the way it swings this way
and that in the pushing and the
pulling.  For, once you have stepped
through the threshold, the knob, like
much of what went on before and will
transpire in the moments ahead

will be forgotten
for all the
noise and pain that suffices for
life and wandering. So, note the ease
and craftsmanship in the place your
hand rests for a hold. Its easy beauty
will be gone like a flash.

Note it well, this thing
that silently establishes the
door's final stroke.

Pay it the homage due a thing
of pure functionality and utter
grace.

Without it you stutter for a way
to grasp what lies between
you and the morrow.  So, hold
it firm—thankfully with

resolute departure in your opening
and in your stride.

## Beneath that Doorframe

Beneath the doorframe
in Mom-mom's house were
those steps, the ones that creaked their way
down to that dirt floor basement.

The creaks themselves betrayed
the presence of forces and beings
that every child knows exist beneath
grey wooden stairs that crawl down
into dirt floor basements of
grandparents houses.

Some days,
some days now,

I can smell the dirt when
opening a door—

any door—
in—
and toward me—
as that door did—in
and toward me.

Sometimes—

the feel of a roughly
pocked
cast-iron knob
turning cold and slippery
in my hand
finds me wandering in thought and
inner scent toward that musty
basement floor; cobwebs and

coal lining the edges of my
aperture.

I knew there were ogres
under that stairway,

I knew with an inner knowing
I could not overthrow. They were
there, and I would run full
throttle up and down those
gray painted wooden stairs whenever
I had to get jars of peaches
from the room on the left,

or take a drink to the one
shoveling the coal.

Avoiding their clutches—

my sole reason
for existence and
movement.

I would not be fooled.
The knowing I held in my
child heart was clear,

these sorts of doors lead
to peril—BEWARE.

The fear of
all the ages –

of your whole lifetime –

is in the heart you hold deep
within as a child,
and the simple things
you find within the clutches
of your own hands.

## THE FINALE

Beneath each
and
every doorframe
I walk through;

and beneath each
and every window
I gaze through,

there is a solidity
of the earth –

a firm place –

on which I stand
and bear my lever
against all odds.

O brindled memory of
youthful play,
leaning into the knowledge
of no sense of time.

Mud flowing freely
between the toes
of the days of abandon
at the foot
of this tree—at the
foot of that tree.

It does not matter
how we bring the earth
up from between our knees.
It may be dirt,
it may be mud,

it may be sand.

O blissful resignation
of giving oneself over
to a lost-ness in the imagination
and intimate fondling
of the very dirt and sand
that builds the atoms of
our who-ness -

stardust and carbon
have screamed their way
across the universe
to build a youthful spleen
that is intoxicated on
merriment and the curve

of a plateful of suspended
disbelief.

Days of dragons
and hideous goblins under the
bed of my ID and EGO,

how have you shaped
my view of board meetings
and competition between
apex, alpha predictors and

malingerers surrounding
the passion of their own
self-love.

Give me the crayfish,
give me the whittled rod
for fishing great urchins of
imagination and flesh out

of the brackish water
of the soul and inland reef of
bitter saturation
and soul-deep brine.

Take me back to
the place where my levered
stance was posed in
joy and mirth—skippingly
entwined with carelessness;

reclined on the un-named
tit of GOD.  I had the lever
planted against the back-drop
of the cosmos as a child holds

How quickly
freedom turns to competition
with the coursing flow
of genes and hormones of aging flesh.

Trading in our playing
in the sand with an uninterrupted
play in the soil of our sex.

Everything here is about bringing
myself into the future by coupling
with the compliment of species

and finding the bliss point of
replication and release splattered

against the back-drop of
radically stated purpose
and osiago twisted in the
bitter herbs of youthful supremacy
of ideals and belief.

O sureness and cockiness
of so feeling the wisdom
of every piece of information
and animate truth from
all time—knowing I know it all
with faultless aperture and

infinite interpretive scope.

All else is wrong.

Every other thought
or feeling leaning into the reticulated
display of the panoply of answers
and infinite regressions of noble truth
is wrong in the rightness of adolescent presence

and assertion.
The adolescent levers
itself
against itself and its
own supreme inflated
understanding of who it
thinks it is.

And, for a span
the lever holds.
Building the ego
large enough
you can leverage
the youthful plumage
against the cosmos and still move
things.

O that line –
that line in the
sand of conflict
and old age.

O that line
that separates the
deep rooted
ego's power
against the universe

is drawn with
sickness, failures,
and the constant pressure
of competition and
compromise.


Can there be a solidness in
mid-life?
Is the place I stand firm once
I have begun to atrophy?

Or,
is it the juxtaposition of what I feel
over and against what I force myself
to believe about my present state and
what is real about reality.

There are times my lever is only
wedged into what I am able to

convince myself is planted
against all odds.

I tell myself all is well,
and believe myself all too easily
in the conspiracy of atrophied will
and compromised integrity.

And yet, I am gaining
a knowledge that says,

pry against your character.
Seek leverage
against your soul.  Stand
firm and take your
lever to the place in you
that is not your ego.

That bedrock,

beyond youthful play,

beyond adolescent pluck,
that empty place in the center
of yourself that is the black hole
of being and non-attachment;

leverage against that place
of emptiness and you
will move the universe
that is the truest.

The way you are and the one
you are that stands and peers out

and walks through.

The fight is not against the
world out there,

it is against the world
in here.  Every passage through
and every peering out is a way
of falling back into
the still center of the
wonder and awe.

www.ingramcontent.com/pod-product-compliance
Lightning Source LLC
Chambersburg PA
CBHW071106090426
42737CB00013B/2500